My Grumpy's Shed

by
Louise Maguire

My Grumpy's Shed
Copyright © 2021 by Louise Maguire

All rights reserved. No part of this publication may be reproduced, distributed, or transmitted in any form or by any means, including photocopying, recording, or other electronic or mechanical methods, without the prior written permission of the author, except in the case of brief quotations embodied in critical reviews and certain other non-commercial uses permitted by copyright law.

Tellwell Talent
www.tellwell.ca

ISBN
978-0-2288-3771-8 (Hardcover)
978-0-2288-3770-1 (Paperback)
978-0-2288-3773-2 (eBook)

To Grumpy,

Love from your girls

When I visit, I love to play in Grumpy's shed.

Grumpy's shed is so big that Nanny says there's more shed than house.

She is really old, even older than Grumpy. When we go for a drive, she moves very, very s...l...o...w...l...y...

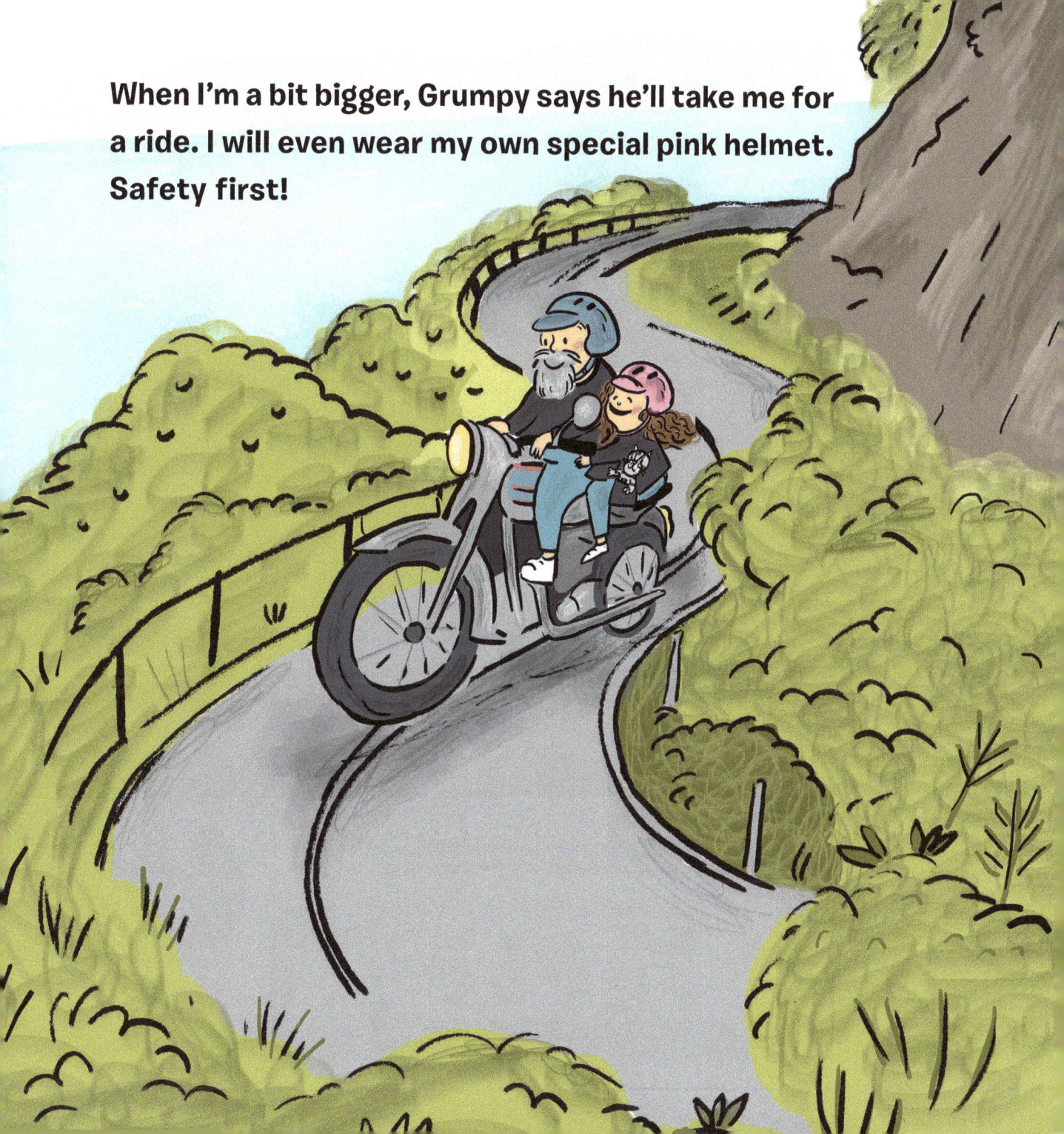

When I'm a bit bigger, Grumpy says he'll take me for a ride. I will even wear my own special pink helmet. Safety first!

In summer, Grumpy takes me to the river and we go skiing on the water. I always remember to wear a life jacket in case I fall in the water!

I jump on Grumpy's knee and help him finish mowing the lawn. He can't finish this huge job without my help.

We pack up the shed and go inside to see what Nanny's made for lunch.

She's made some of her special sausage rolls. Yum!

www.ingramcontent.com/pod-product-compliance
Lightning Source LLC
LaVergne TN
LVHW072016060526
838200LV00059B/4687